AMSTERDAM ⁙ DNA

How Amsterdam became Amsterdam

Amsterdam Museum

Uitgeverij Bas Lubberhuizen

Contents

Introduction

What determines a city's character? Or who indeed? A city is more than just the sum of its architecture and planning over the centuries. Amsterdam is not merely the central canals, the high-rise offices along the motorway or Vondel Park. And the city is more than the sum of all the men, women and children who live here. Of whom there are over 800,000. So what makes Amsterdam such a unique place, so different from other cities?

Understanding Amsterdam means looking back in time. There are four basic ingredients to the city's DNA, which have formed its character over the centuries: enterprise, civic virtue, creativity and freedom of thought. These elements may not always be visible on the surface, and maybe not all at the same time. Yet they have all played a formative role in the course of a thousand years in making Amsterdam what it is today.

Spirit of Enterprise

An essential aspect of Amsterdam's success as a commercial city is the spirit of enterprise of its people. For centuries, they have exhibited a unique sense of commercial endeavour. It is due to this trading instinct that the city has played a key role in many areas of international economic activity. Yet the city has never had a ruling class strong and wealthy enough to extend its domain abroad and so turn the country into an international power. Amsterdam's entrepreneurs act collectively. Hence the creation of the first joint stock company and multinational corporation: the Dutch East India Company (VOC).

Civic Virtue

Combined commercial enterprise also brings a typical feature of Amsterdam society to the fore: as soon as people are wealthy enough to afford it, they are expected to help the disadvantaged - a kind of social welfare *avant la lettre*. After all, successful burghers also once started from the same modest beginnings. Indeed, social unrest in the city would be bad for trade! A nice example of wealthy burghers caring for the underprivileged is the former Civic Orphanage, which has housed Amsterdam Museum since 1975.

Creativity

Amsterdam's creativity is visually evident in the Amsterdam DNA show, in work by artists as diverse as Rembrandt and Marlene Dumas, as well as in the city's roots. To build on this marshy soil requires deep foundations. A small country with little land and raw materials has to be inventive to be able to compete with more powerful nations round about and further afield. In its constant search for innovation, Amsterdam has managed to compensate for its deficiencies. This starts in the Middle Ages with the development of faster freight ships and continues today with the construction of the world's biggest Internet exchange point, here in Amsterdam.

Freedom of Thought

Innovation requires thinking outside the box, unhampered by traditional methods and techniques. And there is another reason why Amsterdam has acquired a worldwide reputation (for better or worse) for freedom of ideas: Amsterdam has exported its commercial spirit across the globe and the whole world comes to

The Governesses of the Civic Orphanage, 1683
Adriaen Backer (1635/36–1684)

Amsterdam's door. If you want to do business with strangers, you have to respect them and their customs when you meet. With the positive corollary that those strangers also turn out to be enterprising, otherwise they would never have come. Moreover, they bring new ideas and ventures, which again stimulates the city's innovative culture.

There is no specific sequence in these four elements of Amsterdam's DNA, although there is clearly a sense of cause and effect: each component stimulates the other. History shows that Amsterdam is successful when all four of elements are given free rein. These are the times that we recall as a Golden Age: the seventeenth century, the late nineteenth century and for some also the 1970s. If one or more of these elements declines, then the city and its inhabitants find themselves in trouble. Today, for example, it is freedom of thought and civic virtue that are under fire. And yet, compared to other cities, Amsterdam is still a city where ideas are discussed freely and where citizens are engaged.

Amsterdam DNA tells the story of around a thousand years of history with reference to the historical objects and art at Amsterdam Museum. It is the story of burghers, entrepreneurs, creative people and free thinkers, of how Amsterdam became Amsterdam.

Paul Spies, Amsterdam Museum director

c. 1306 1306 Amsterdam receives town charter.

Pilgrim's badge, c. 1500

1345 The Miracle of Amsterdam turns Amsterdam into a place of pilgrimage. Pilgrims buy trinkets as souvenirs. This badge shows the sacramental wafer held up by two angels.

Miracle

In March 1345, a miracle occurs on Kalverstraat. A dying man is given the last rites. He is so ill however, that he is unable to keep the sacramental wafer down. The maid throws his vomit on the fire, and in the morning there it is, like new: the wafer, unburned. A priest brings the undigested wafer to St Nicholas church (today's Oude Kerk). Amazingly, the wafer returns to the dead man's house. Twice. The miracle is confirmed by the Holy See in Rome.

On the site of the miracle, on Kalverstraat, a chapel is built: Heilige Stede. Pilgrims come to Amsterdam from far and wide. In fact the Miracle stimulates the economic expansion of Amsterdam as well as its religious growth in the later Middle Ages. Most illustrious of all the pilgrims is Maximilian of Austria. His imperial crown becomes part of the heraldic emblem of Amsterdam, thanks not least to the Miracle.

Amsterdam's coat of arms

NAP

Amsterdam's water level is the oldest standard of its kind: **Normaal Amsterdams Peil** (NAP). All water level measurements in the Netherlands are set by NAP, and in much of Europe too. Amsterdam's city hall has a presentation on the history of NAP. Open Thursday to Saturday.

Below the Surface

This is part of the wooden foundation of a house on Herengracht. Without wooden piles Amsterdam would sink into the mud – today too.

Foundation, 17th century

1489 Maximilian of Austria allows Amsterdam to use his royal (later imperial) crown in the city's heraldic emblem.

A Squad of Harquebusiers with Two Champion Marksmen, 1534
Unknown artist

Security in the City

In the later Middle Ages the militiamen of the longbow- and crossbowmen's guilds keep the peace in Amsterdam and defend the city. In 1522, another civic-guard guild is formed, using firearms: harquebuses. The men in the centre at the front are wearing livery collars awarded to the best marksmen. They are the winners of the annual shooting competition.

1535 Anabaptist Riots.

In the courtyard at **Begijnhof** stands a famous wooden house (no. 34), built around 1528. It is the oldest building in Holland with a wooden facade. Another wooden house on Zeedijk (no. 1) dates from slightly later. After a huge fire engulfed the town in 1452, the burgesses ruled that dividing walls should henceforth be made of brick. In 1669, the rule was extended to facades as well.

Stories in the Soil

Remains from the past are found at every excavation site. Some are quite recent, others are hundreds of years old. Perishable materials such as wood and leather, which would disintegrate elsewhere, remain relatively well-preserved in the marshy soil on which Amsterdam is built. These finds tell us about the lives of ordinary people. They were never meant to last for ever, which makes it all the more extraordinary that they have survived.

Bone carder, c. 1150

Skate, c. 1240

Boat hook, first half 14th century

Leather sheath, early 14th century

1000–1550

Cooking pot,
14th century

Wooden spoon, second half
14th century

Crucifix, 15th century

Toy knucklebone, from a
jacks set, 15th century

Pincer, 14th century

1550–1600

1566 Religious Riots/
Iconoclasm.

Revolt against King and Church

Jan Micker's *Bird's-Eye View of Amsterdam* looks like an aerial picture, full of detail (see page 18-19). As if the artist had drawn it from a balloon, brush in hand, although of course balloons had not been invented yet. The shadows cast by the clouds give the painting a spectacular, modern effect.

This is Amsterdam in the mid-sixteenth century. The north faces down. That emphasises the harbour. Large seafaring ships lie at anchor on the IJ. Smaller craft are carrying goods to and from the city's warehouses. All around there are churches and monasteries. This is a Catholic city, part of the sprawling Habsburg Empire. And big changes are about to happen.

In 1578, Amsterdam expels its Catholic hierarchy and withdraws its allegiance from Philip II in Madrid. The Dutch are fighting for their independence: the Eighty Years War (1568-1648). Amsterdam is the last town in Holland to declare for William of Orange and throw in its lot with the revolt against Spanish dominion over the Low Countries. In a peaceful coup, Amsterdam's

Amsterdam's **Oude Kerk** is the city's oldest building. There was a wooden chapel on this site in the thirteenth century. Originally Catholic, in 1578 it was seized and turned into a Protestant church. Today, besides being a house of prayer, it is also a concert hall and exhibition space.
→ www.oudekerk.nl

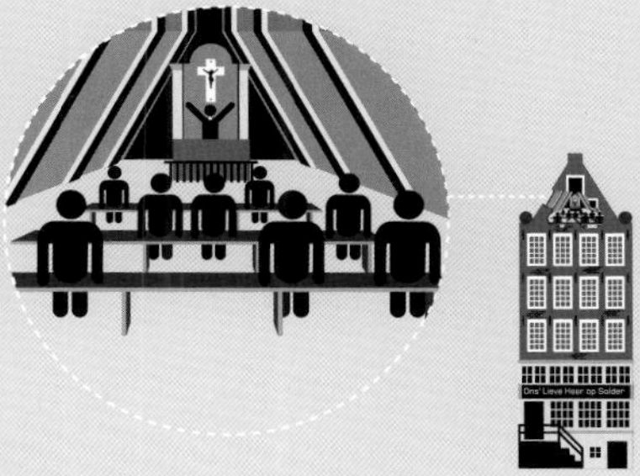

After 1578, Amsterdam's Catholics had to keep their religious practices private. In 1661, Jan Hartman built **a secret church** in the attic of his house on Oudezijds Voorburgwal (no. 40). The church has survived intact and is now a museum, Our Lord in the Attic. → www.opsolder.nl

leading Protestants take over the reins of power. The deposed clergy and burgesses are escorted to waiting barges and sent into exile. Yet the Alteration, as the takeover is known, is not entirely nonviolent. As many a disfigured altarpiece and smashed statue testify.

In the southern provinces, the war continues. In 1585, Antwerp falls to the Spaniards. When the Dutch blockade the River Scheldt, its harbour is cut off from the sea. Ships, people and capital flock from the Southern Netherlands to the north. Amsterdam becomes the economic hub of the new Dutch Republic. This is the dawn of the Golden Age.

Start of Eighty Years War against Philip II of Spain. **1568**

Bird's-Eye View of Amsterdam, c. 1652–1655, Jan Micker (1598–1664)

Bird's-Eye View of Amsterdam, 1538, Cornelis Anthonisz. (c. 1505–1553)

Bird's-Eye View of Amsterdam, c. 1652–1655

Micker has painted the city as it looked around 1540, long before it acquires its ring of canals. It is based on the *Bird's-Eye View* that Cornelis Anthonisz made in 1538, the earliest known map of Amsterdam.

Eighty Years War

In the year 1568, rebellion breaks out in the Low Countries against the Spanish king, Philip II. His commander in the field, the Duke of Alva, attempts to crush the Dutch with an iron fist. Resistance grows, led by Prince William of Orange. Alva's ruthless suppression of Protestant heretics is a major reason for this increasing support for the Revolt. The Spaniards allow only Catholicism; some Protestants are even burned at the stake.

One by one, the cities of Holland join the Revolt, yet Amsterdam continues to support Philip and Alva. Soon the city is isolated: a small Catholic enclave in a sea of insurgency. In 1578, ten years into the war, Amsterdam finally declares for William of Orange. After which the city grows at an unprecedented pace, thanks not least to the blockade of rival Antwerp's harbour. The war ends in 1648 in a Dutch triumph: the Republic of the United Provinces emerges independent, and ... Protestant.

Innocent Victim

This sculpture was found at an excavation in 1984. It is a Pieta: it shows the Virgin Mary mourning as she cradles the body of her dead son Jesus Christ. The work once stood in the chapel of St Gertrude's monastery. It was probably during the Alteration in 1578 that Jesus and Mary's faces were chiselled away. Religious statues were considered idolatrous by Protestants.

Alteration 1578

This ox starts life as a witness to the Adoration of the Shepherds at the stable in Bethlehem. Two of the shepherds can be seen leaning forward. The panel is a fragment, probably from a large Nieuwe Kerk altarpiece. Presumably it was broken up during the rioting that accompanied the Alteration in 1578. This section is all that survives.

Adoration of the Shepherds (fragment), c. 1559. Pieter Aertsen (1507–1575)

Piëta, c. 1450
Artist unknown

Protagonists

For years, William of Orange (1533-1584) tries to win Amsterdam over to the Revolt against Philip II of Spain (1527–1598). Unlike the rest of Holland's cities, Amsterdam remains a refuge and supplier for the Spanish troops in the province. The Duke of Alva (1507–1582), the ruthless Spanish general, lodges here temporarily to coordinate his campaign.

William of Orange, c. 1582. After Adriaen Thomasz Key

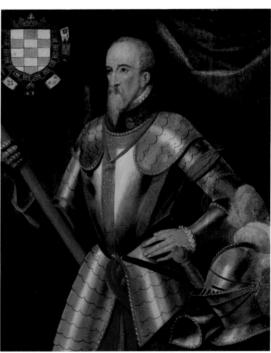

Fernando Alvarez de Toledo, Duke of Alva, second half 16th century. Artist unknown

Thomas Gerritsz Doesburch, Claesje Hendricksdr Roeclaes and their Two Daughters, 1559. Jacob War II (d. 1568), attributed

St Lucia Convent becomes Civic Orphanage (now Amsterdam Museum).

1580

This plaque is from the entrance on Kalverstraat.

Exile

Grain merchant Thomas Gerritsz Doesburch (1532–before 1579) and his wife Claesje Rooclaes (1539–1562) commission this portrait shortly after they marry. The two daughters are added after their mother's death. In 1567, Doesburch is one of the leaders of the Protestant burghers against the Catholic burgesses. He is expelled from the city and supports the Revolt from exile in Antwerp.

A House for God's Word

Pious congregants listen attentively to the preacher's words in Amsterdam's Oude Kerk. Until 1578, this church is dedicated to St Nicholas, the city's patron saint. When the Protestants take over, the name disappears and the interior is ransacked. Idolatrous statues and altars are removed. Henceforth, congregants focus their attention on the new pulpit, in the middle of the church.

Interior of Oude Kerk, 1661. Emanuel de Witte (c. 1617–1692)

Jan Pietersz Sweelinck, 1606. Gerrit Pietersz Sweelinck (1566–after 1612)

Antwerp is sacked by **1585**
the Spaniards. Rebels
from the northern
provinces block the River
Scheldt and bring
Antwerp's flourishing
trade to a halt. People,
expertise and capital
flock to Amsterdam.

Orpheus on the Amstel

Composer, organist and harpsichordist Jan Pietersz Sweelinck (1562–1621) is born a Catholic. He is plays the organ at the pre-Alteration Oude Kerk. After 1578, he gives free weekday concerts there. Sweelinck's improvisations and his virtuosity earn him the name of 'Orpheus on the Amstel'. He influences generations of composers, including Johann Sebastian Bach.

World at her Feet

In 1606, Pieter Isaacsz decorates a harpsichord for the town hall. Below Amsterdam's heraldic emblem sits the city, surrounded by surfeit and shipping.

Allegory of Amsterdam as the Centre of World Trade, 1606
Pieter Isaacsz (1569–1625)

Civic Guards

Portraits of civic guards usually depict members of a single company that patrols the streets of a neighbourhood. Here the commander, Captain Jacob Gerritsz Hoing (1555–1625), presents his company of guardsmen. Standing left of centre, he turns towards us, gesturing with his hand. In his other hand he holds a pikestaff, the traditional weapon of a company captain.

Jan Bicker and Agniet de Graeff, c. 1663–64
Jan Lievens (1607–1674) after Wallerand Vaillant (1623–1677)

Pieter Jansz Reael, 1643
Govert Flinck (1615–1660)

Hiob de Wildt, 1640
Dirck van Santvoort
(1610–1680)

The Governesses and Matrons of the Spinhuis, 1638
Dirck van Santvoort (1610–1680)

1632 Athenaeum Illustre
founded, precursor of
Amsterdam University.

Women Only

Thieves, prostitutes and loose women are imprisoned in
the women's workhouse, or Spinhuis. Here they learn to
spin wool and other handicrafts. One of the governesses
is inspecting lace.

Registration of the Poor and Orphans at the Almshouse, 1626
Unknown artist

Without Prejudice

An almshouse is established in 1613 'to prevent all
manner of abuse in this prosperous city, and to keep
the beggars off the streets'. Here food is distributed and
the poor, foundlings and orphans can register for aid.
It makes no difference what their background is. The
governors are shown in this portrait performing their
charitable work.

Treaty of Munster ends **1648**
the Eighty Years War.

Allegory of the Care of Lepers and Innocents, c. 1675
Gérard de Lairesse (1641–1711)

1655 The new town hall on Dam Square opens.

This construction model of the new town hall was made in 1648. The building is the largest in the Republic. Poet Joost van den Vondel calls it the Eighth Wonder of the World. Design: Jacob van Campen (1595-1657)

Virtuous Ceiling

Eight allegorical scenes on the ceiling of the Leper House boardroom summarise the institution's tasks. Abundance points to the clouds to show a poor woman the source of her prosperity: Religio.

Centre of Town

Crowds are milling about on Dam Square: workmen, burghers and merchants, everyone is out and about. The recently completed town hall dominates the scene. At the weigh house, on the right, quantities are being measured. Small freight boats line the bank of Damrak canal, since filled in. To the right is a sleigh, a coach without wheels that is dragged over the cobblestones.

Dam Square, 1675, Abraham Storck (1644–1708)

Expanding Amsterdam

In 1657, the city decides to launch a fourth major expansion. Here Amsterdam is showing a map to the divine Jupiter and his wife Juno. The city's characteristic semicircular shape is discernable.

Allegory of the Expansion of
Amsterdam, c. 1663
Nicolaes Berchem (1620–1683)

The Herengracht Bend, 1685, Gerrit Berckheyde (1638–1698)

1672 **Disaster Year: the Republic is attacked by France, Britain, Munster and Cologne.**

Golden Bend

A sunny day on Herengracht in 1685. The houses along the canal have recently been completed, following the city's recent expansion. Now the three main canals continue to the River Amstel. This section of Herengracht is the most expensive part of the canal. To allow an uninterrupted view of the new buildings, Berckheyde has left out the young trees that line the canal.

1600–1700

Daniel Bernard, 1669, Bartholomeus van der Helst (1613–1670)

Merchant of Amsterdam

Daniel Bernard (1626–1714) views the artist with confidence, and indeed anyone else who may be looking. Bernard ships and trades in Russia, Spain, Italy and the Levant. The papers he has just signed refer to the Dutch East India Company (voc), of which his father is a director. Doubtless he hopes one day to follow in the old man's footsteps.

Suriname Society **1683** founded; Amsterdam becomes a joint owner of Suriname.

The Gouden Leeuw on the IJ, 1686
Willem van de Velde II (1633–1707)

Embarking for the East

A smack is leaving the jetty at Montelbaan tower. On board, sailors who have signed up for a minimum of five years service in the Dutch East India Company (voc). Soldiers are also enlisted. Like the sailors, most are foreign. Their job is to defend the Asian trading posts. The boat brings the men to the huge eastindiamen anchored off Texel, where their long voyage begins.

Embarkation of Company Troops at Montelbaan Tower, 1682
Abraham Storck (1644–after 1704)

Working at the Shipyard

Bakhuizen has incorporated all the principal tasks carried out at the voc shipyard in this picture. A half-finished eastindiaman has just been launched onto the water. On the left is a voc ship almost ready for its maiden voyage. In the background stands the colossal 180-metre wide maritime depot where supplies and victuals are stored (today's Maritime Museum).

The Shipyard of the Dutch East India Company (VOC), 1696
Ludolf Bakhuizen (1630–1708)

Lively Day at the Exchange

Since it opened in 1611, the stock exchange on Rokin near Dam Square is a meeting place for Dutch and international merchants and brokers. In addition to an array of products, people also trade in stocks, bonds and other financial certificates. In 1668–70 the stock exchange expands in response to the growth in economic activity. The new section is shown here.

The Courtyard of Amsterdam's Stock Exchange, c. 1670–1680
Job Berckheyde (1630–1693)

 Peter the Great visits Amsterdam. 1683

Tsar Peter the Great (1672–1725) is determined to modernise Russia. To gather intelligence he tours Europe, and stays in Amsterdam. He works as a carpenter at the VOC shipyard.

Peter the Great, 18th century
Unknown artist

Beauty and Splendour

It is not just in painting that Amsterdam excels. Gold- and silversmiths also produce exquisite masterpieces. Engravers design magnificent glass drinking vessels to mark special occasions. Huge sums are paid for fine ceramic pieces and beautifully decorated exotic objects.

Delftware tulip vase, c. 1700
Unknown maker

Silver spice box, 1618
Willem van Wolfswinkel
(fl. 1591–1626)

Silver funeral shield of the corn meters' guild, 1633
Johannes Lutma I
(1584–1669)

Silver pleated dish, 1662
Mijndert Takel (1638–1707)

Silver salt cellar, 1643
Johannes Lutma I (1584–1669)

Silver sconce, c. 1680
Unknown maker

Nautilus cup, 1649
Hendrick Bloem (1619–1659)

Mother-of-pearl shell,
second half 17th century
Cornelis Bellekin
(1615–1696)

Turbo shell, second half 17th
century
Unknown maker

Cash is King

The exchange bank at the town hall is one of the world's oldest banks. Special money wagons are used to transport the heavy coin chests which are tugged back and forth with a block and tackle on rails.

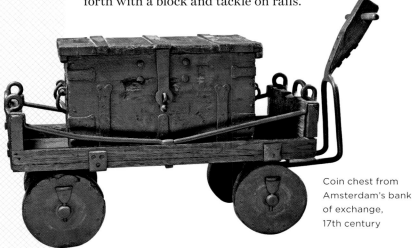

Coin chest from
Amsterdam's bank
of exchange,
17th century

A Portuguese in Amsterdam

Antonio Lopes Suasso (1614–1685) is a descendant of Portuguese Jews, refugees from the Iberian peninsula who found a safe haven in free Amsterdam. Suasso is one of Europe's leading merchants and bankers, and a confidant of Stadholder-King William III.

Antonio Lopes Suasso, c. 1685
Rombout Verhulst (1674–1698),
attributed

1600–1700

Groundbreaking Art and Science

Each year the surgeons' guild holds a public anatomical demonstration using the cadaver of an executed criminal. Rembrandt's Anatomy Lesson shows Dr Jan Deijman (1619-1666) dissecting the brain of the dead man. An assistant is holding part of the skull in his hand. This is a fragment of the original painting, most of which was lost in a fire in 1723.

The Anatomy Lesson of Dr Jan Deijman, 1656
Rembrandt van Rijn (1606–1669)

Calm between Storms

The eighteenth century is a period of relative calm in Amsterdam, although not for everyone, and certainly not for those caught in the crossfire. Yet in retrospect, the unprecedented dynamic and innovation of the Golden Age seems to have evaporated.

Not that the Republic is in trouble. Just that Dutch trade no longer dominates the world, and Dutch foreign policy no longer carries the same weight it once had. Britain and France have caught up and left Holland standing. For almost a century, Amsterdam had been the centre of the world. Now the focus has shifted.

In Amsterdam, the big money moves away from commodities and into finance. The city of enterprise and venture turns into a city of bankers. One name stands out: Hope & Co on Keizersgracht, originally Scottish, the company emerges as one of Europe's largest banks.

As elsewhere in Europe, the ideals of the Enlightenment begin to find adherents in Amsterdam: reason and progress are the watchwords in science, education, social reform and politics. In 1777, a group of wealthy Amsterdam burghers establish Felix Meritis (happiness through merit): a club to promote art and science. This century of change culminates in a revolution in France (1789) which sweeps across Europe and shakes Amsterdam to its core..

1702
Willem III dies, following a riding accident.
Start of the Second Stadholderless Period. Amsterdam's burgomasters regain the right to appoint the city's magistrates.

The magnificent **Felix Meritis** building on Keizersgracht is a venue for art, culture and science since 1777.
→ www.felixmeritis.nl

Little Dolls for Grown-up Women

It is not just children who play with dolls in the eighteenth century: it is a hobby for ladies too. And an opportunity to show off their wealth in elegant fashion. The number of miniature silver objects is astonishing. Most are the work of Arnoldus van Geffen (1728–1769), a silversmith in Amsterdam. His silver trinkets are minor masterpieces.

Dolls house with miniature silver, c. 1730–70

Repeal of WIC's trading monopoly in the West Indies. **1734**

Greek Myth in Amsterdam

This silver shell box combines the skills of craftsmen from two different centuries. The lid and bottom are made of mother-of-pearl shells. These were decorated in the seventeenth century by Cornelis Bellekin, a famous engraver. Decades later, the Amsterdam jeweller Louis Métayer incorporates them in a box. The lid shows Perseus rescuing the bound Andromeda.

1747
1748
Doelist riots in Amsterdam. A new city council is appointed.

Box with two mother-of-pearl shells, engraved 1650-1700, silver 1741
Cornelis Bellekin (1615–1696) and Louis Métayer (fl. 1730–1774)

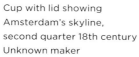
Cup with lid showing
Amsterdam's skyline,
second quarter 18th century
Unknown maker

Cup showing the *Admiraal de Ruyter*,
second half eighteenth century
Unknown maker

Yesterday's Glory

In the eighteenth century, the Dutch begin to look back
with nostalgia at the Golden Age. This glass shows an
eastindiaman in full sail: a ship of the once mighty
Dutch East India Company which collapses in 1798.
An inscription on the glass reads: to the success of the
Admiral de Ruyter. The ship is named after one of the
naval heroes of the previous century.

1772 Municipal theatre on Keizersgracht, built by Jacob van Campen, burns down completely. Only the entrance survives. Eighteen people die.

Free to Build

Jews first arrive in Amsterdam in the late sixteenth century. Many others follow, finding a safe haven from persecution. By the late eighteenth century, a tenth of the city's population is Jewish. Two of Amsterdam's synagogues stand out: on the left stands the Ashkenazi New Synagogue and Great Synagogue; on the right behind the trees is the Portuguese Esnoga.

View of Houtmarkt, c. 1760–1787, Hendrik Keun (1738–1787)

There were few places in Europe where Jews could live and practice their faith as openly as in Amsterdam in the seventeenth and eighteenth century. On Jonas Daniël Meijerplein the **Portuguese Synagogue**, completed in 1675, is open to the public. Across the road, the Ashkenazi synagogue complex now houses the **Jewish Historical Museum**. ➡ www.portugesesynagoge.nl ➡ www.jhm.nl

1795–1815

Liberty, Equality, Fraternity

In 1795, six years into the French Revolution, Napoleon's armies march into Holland, with the support of Amsterdam's revolutionary Patriot party. Three years later, Holland has its first written constitution based an unprecedented radical concept: equal rights for all. The revolutionary slogan is 'Liberty, Equality, Fraternity'. While in practice, there is still a long way to go, this marks the start of democracy in the Netherlands.

French tricolours fly over Dam Square. A few years back, the town hall was the proud bastion of Amsterdam's burghers; the French occupation has turned all that around. Since 1808, the town hall is the palace of Louis Bonaparte, the first king of Holland – a Frenchman. The Dutch Republic is history.

Yet Louis has only a few years to enjoy his new home. His elder brother, Napoleon Bonaparte, dispenses with his services and annexes Holland. On 9 October 1811, the emperor comes to receive the symbolic keys to the city, here Van Bree shows him riding a white horse. The French Empire now extends to Amsterdam, its third capital, after Paris and Rome. Under the French, all kinds of modernisations are introduced, yet the economy collapses. This is above all due to the Continental System: the French ban on

1795 **Batavian Republic proclaimed.**

contact with British ships and traders around the world. By the time the French evacuate Amsterdam in 1813, the city is reduced to poverty.

Arrival of Napoleon in Amsterdam, c. 1811–12
Mattheus Ignatius van Bree (1773–1839)

Imperial Welcome

Riding a white horse, Emperor Napoleon enters Dam Square. An honorary guard of mounted officers lines the square, keeping the crowd at a safe distance. After the emperor's visit, the square is given a new name: Place Napoleon.

Dancing around the Liberty Tree on Dam Square, 19 June 1795
Jonas Zeuner (1727–1814)

1808 Town hall converted into a palace for Louis Bonaparte. Amsterdam becomes the Dutch capital.

Freedom Dance in Silver and Gold

On 19 July 1795, people are dancing around the Liberty Tree on Dam Square. A bonnet and streamer adorn the decorated pole. The pro-French Patriot party has proclaimed the Batavian Republic. This strengthens the country's ties with revolutionary France. Jonas Zeuner has recorded the celebrations using a special method: engraving gold and silver leaf on glass.

On 9 October 1811, Emperor Napoleon entered Amsterdam through **Muiderpoort**. The gate was decorated to form a triumphal arch for the occasion. It stood at the edge of town until well into the nineteenth century. The edifice has long since been swallowed up by the expanding city, where Sarphatistraat meets Plantage Middenlaan (near the Tropenmuseum).

Child of the Revolution

After the French Revolution, Napoleon Bonaparte (1769–1821) emerges as the most powerful man in Europe. He extends France's borders ever further, eventually annexing the new Batavian Republic. His reign comes to an end at the Battle of Waterloo in 1815.

Bust of Napoleon
Bonaparte, c. 1808
Antoine-Denis Chaudet
(1763–1810)

Emperor Napoleon visits Amsterdam

Between 1810 and 1813, Holland forms part of imperial France, with Amsterdam as its third capital. Napoleon pays one visit to the city in this period, in October 1811. To mark the occasion, Amsterdam's burgomasters offer him these symbolic keys on a red velvet cushion.

Keys to the city of Amsterdam, 1811
Diederik Lodewijk Bennewitz (1763–1826)

Louis Bonaparte, 1808
Charles Howard Hodges (1764–1837)

French King of Holland

In 1806, the French emperor Napoleon appoints his brother king of Holland. Louis Bonaparte (1778–1846) is determined to forge a united Dutch nation. Here he is wearing the uniform of a Dutch colonel, with the Grand Cross of the Royal Order of the Union.

Mighty as an Eagle

In 1811, Napoleon enters Amsterdam along Plantage Middenlaan. A triumphal arch is erected there, decorated with a gilded eagle. The eagle has been a symbol of imperial power since Roman times.

Eagle, 1811
Maker unknown

Napoleon had enormous barracks built in Amsterdam. The complex, based on the French model, was 276 metres long and could house 2,400 men. After Napoleon's defeat, the French imperial emblem was quickly replaced by an Orange heraldic symbol. Today, **Orange-Nassau barracks** house offices and apartments. It is on Sarphatistraat, opposite Artis.

Execution at Nieuwmarkt

One of the innovations that the French bring to the Netherlands is the guillotine. It is only used once in Amsterdam, on 15 June 1812. Three heads roll that day.

Model of a guillotine, early 19th century
Unknown maker

Enlightened Propaganda

On 19 July 1795, a day after Orangist stadholder Willem V flees, the Batavian Republic is proclaimed. In Amsterdam the first assembly representatives are elected. To celebrate, various monuments depicting symbolic scenes are erected around the city. These are illuminated at night, although strong winds extinguish many of the oil lamps.

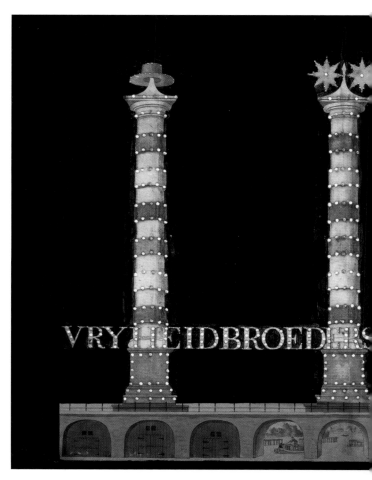

At Hogesluis on the River Amstel, three columns proclaim the revolutionary ideals. Liberty is symbolised by a hat, Fraternity by twin stars and Equality by a triangular compass.

Liberty, Fraternity, Equality, 1795
D.M. Langeveld (publisher)

Napoleon is defeated, 1813
Willem I takes the
Dutch throne.

1815–1870

Poverty and Civic Duty

When the French leave Amsterdam, the city is 22 million guilders in debt. The half century that follows is a time of poverty and ill health. The city's power has crumbled away. While Amsterdam may be the capital in name, it is in The Hague that political power resides in the new kingdom of the Netherlands. Moreover, Rotterdam harbour is an expanding economic competitor. And on the world stage, Amsterdam has long since dropped out of view.

Halfway into the nineteenth century, Amsterdam is an impoverished town with its canals reduced to foul-smelling sewers. Yet Amsterdam has a bourgeois class too, and in addition to looking after themselves they are also conscious of their civic duty. They promote culture and nature among the townspeople. As the century progresses, they introduce public services: for example Artis Zoo (1838), Vondel Park (1865) and Concertgebouw concert hall (1888).

Perhaps the greatest of these nineteenth-century philanthropists is Samuel Sarphati, a Jewish doctor in Amsterdam. He campaigns against the unhygienic conditions (and stench!) by installing public toilets, and by organising a rubbish collection service. His most spectacular project is the Palace of Industry (1864), a magnificent steel and glass edifice inspired by London's Crystal Palace. It is eventually destroyed by a huge fire in 1929. In 1968, the remains of this people's palace on Frederiksplein are replaced by an impregnable Dutch Central Bank.

1825   **North Holland Canal is built.**

1838   **Natura Artis Magistra founded: today's Artis Zoo.**

Parade at Hogesluis towards the Palace of Industry, undated
Unknown photographer, Amsterdam Municipal Archive

First rail link **1839**
between
Amsterdam and
Haarlem.

Former Splendour

Sarphati's famous Palace of Industry is designed by
architect Cornelis Outshoorn (1810–1875). He is also the
architect who designs another of Sarphati's celebrated
projects: Amstel Hotel.

Abraham and Louisa Willet-Holthuysen owned a huge
house on Herengracht (no. 605) in the second half of the
nineteenth century. The top floor, with its ballroom and
dining room, gives an impression of the atmosphere in
which well-heeled Amsterdammers live in this period.
Museum Willet-Holthuysen is open to the public daily.
→ www.willetholthuysen.nl

Construction of Two Gasholders at Hollandsche Gazfabriek on Weteringschans, 1847
Cornelis Springer (1817–1891)

1853 A fountain at Haarlemmerplein offers Amsterdammers water piped in from the dunes.

Old and New

Gas, derived from coal, is the new fuel for light and heat. Two Hollandsche Gazfabriek gasholders are located on the outskirts of the city. They are still under construction here. The old town wall is obsolete as a defensive bulwark. In the background, the windmills on the embankment bear testimony to a bygone age.

1864 Palace of Industry opens.

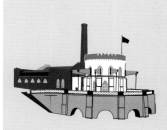

Cruquius, and its sister steam pumps Leeghwater and Lijnden, emptied 800 million cubic metres of water from Haarlemer lake between 1849 and 1852. Until 1912 these engines kept the drained lake dry; then electric pumps took over. The old pump station is now a museum.
→ www.museumdecruquius.nl

Horse in the Water!

Coaches, carts and even trams are drawn by horses. Accidents will happen, and sometimes horses fall into the canal. Butcher J.C. Sinck develops a special hoist to rescue them. Animals that do not survive the ordeal find their way into his butcher shop.

Anna Heineken uses this silver trowel to lay the foundation stone of her son, Gerard Heineken's new brewery.
The wooden trowel box symbolises the new factory.

1867

Trowel and box, 1867

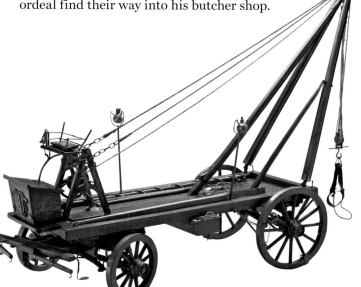

Model of Sinck's hoist, c. 1860

1870–1940

Towards a Modern City

Following a period of relative stagnation, the city starts to regain its momentum around 1870. The Industrial Revolution may have begun late in the Netherlands - compared with Britain and Belgium - but the pace soon picks up. The economy flourishes, due not least to the exploitation of the colonies. In science and culture the city also experiences a renaissance. From a cramped, impoverished town, Amsterdam is soon transformed into a modern metropolis.

New suburbs emerge around the old city centre, built on millions of foundation piles. The sound of pile drivers fills the air. George Hendrik Breitner, painter and photographer, is fascinated by the modern city and portrays the construction work. In his Building Site, a horse is dragging timber to a construction site somewhere in Amsterdam. On the right, a modern pile-driver is hammering foundations into the ground using steam power.

Since the buildings must be above all cheap and easy to construct, the new working-class homes provide appalling living conditions. Entire families live in a single room. This leads to protest, spearheaded by socialists. New political parties and trades unions demand education, jobs and decent housing for all. Inspired by these modern ideals, early in the twentieth century a new architectural style emerges: Amsterdam School.

1876 North Sea Canal opens.

1883 First world exhibition in Amsterdam: International Colonial Exhibition.

While old windmills continue to turn, modern facto-
ries appear alongside. Steamships sail up the new
North Sea Canal (1876) into Amsterdam harbour. A
rapidly expanding rail network links the capital to the
rest of the country, and to all Europe. Trams are no
longer drawn by horses, they are powered by elec-
tricity. Bicycles and cars appear. In 1916, Schiphol
Airport opens and brings the whole world within
reach.

Concertgebouw opens. **1888**

Building Site, c. 1890–1910
George Hendrik Breitner (1857–1923)

Central Station begins **1889**
operating.

Westergasfabriek gas factory was built alongside Haarlemmertrekvaart canal in 1883, fuelling light in Amsterdam's streets and houses. The terrain included gas holders, coal bunkers and a water tower. In recent years the area and the buildings have been thoroughly renovated. Wester Park is now a busy recreation area, while the buildings host a mixture of culture and entertainment.
→ www.westergasfabriek.nl

1894 First Dutch trade union of diamond workers: Algemene Nederlandse Diamant-bewerkersbond.

Welfare City, Welfare State

While the city is changing at a fast tempo, so too is the role of the municipality. Councilors such as Wim Treub (1858–1931) and Floor Wibaut (1859–1936) have a major impact on the everyday life of the people of Amsterdam. The former is a liberal, the latter a socialist. Yet both strive for the same thing: better conditions for ordinary people. To this end, the municipality begins to play a wider role. Essential services such as gas, water and telephone are taken over by the city.

It is in Amsterdam that the first attempts are made to introduce the welfare state, for which Holland will become famous in the second half of the twentieth century. To combat substandard housing, the city builds thousands of new homes, in cooperation with the various housing associations. New working-class areas emerge one after another and Amsterdam gains a reputation as a Mecca for working-class housing.

The Mouth of North Sea Canal at IJmuiden, 1878
Christiaan Dommershuizen (1842–1928)

Full Speed Ahead!

A tug is leading a frigate through the locks at IJmuiden into the open sea. This is the new link between Amsterdam's harbour and the North Sea. Ships of the Netherlands Steamship Company (NSM) first begin using the North Sea Canal in 1879. The voyage to Batavia takes only three weeks by steamer, compared to the five months that a sailing vessel requires.

Ajax football club founded.

1900

In 1903, shipping concern Koninklijke Nederlandse Stoomboot-Maatschappij (KNSM) moved into Amsterdam's eastern harbour: Oostelijk Havengebied. Originally marked by little more than a pier in the IJ, soil extracted to build the North Sea Canal was used to create a new island. From here ocean liners set sail for the colonies. In the 1990s, **KNSM island** became a residential area.

Floor Wibaut (1859–1936) is Amsterdam's first social democratic councilor in charge of finance and housing. He demolishes slums and builds entire new neighbourhoods. His campaign slogan 'Who builds? Wibaut!' still resonates among Amsterdam's older generation.

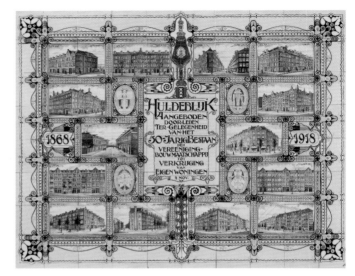

De Key building society tile panel, c. 1918
Plateelbakkerij Delft N.V.

Floor Wibaut, 1934
Tjipke Visser (1876–1955)

Social Housing in Glaze

This tile panel marks the jubilee of the *Bouwmaatschappij tot verkrijging van eigen woningen*. Building societies work successfully to improve housing standards for ordinary households in the second half of the nineteenth century. The tile panel shows fourteen housing blocks built by the society between 1868 and 1918. These are certainly solidly built: almost all still stand today.

Destruction and Construction

Sculptor Frits Sieger is a dedicated communist. This relief symbolises the destruction of the old order and the construction of a new society.

Destruction and Construction, 1930
Frits Sieger (1893–1990)

Olympic Games in Amsterdam. **1928**

Great Depression

Following the Wall Street Crash of 1929 in New York, a major economic depression engulfs the world. In Amsterdam the effect is severe. Tens of thousands lose their job and are left to support themselves and their family from a meagre government benefit. In July 1934, the situation is in danger of exploding. When the government announces a reduction in support, riots break out. Angry unemployed protestors go on the rampage. It takes four days for the police to subdue the Jordaan riots, as the protests are known, and not without help from the army.

Jordaan riots. **1934**

In 1935, as the Great Depression reaches its peak, 60,000 people are unemployed in Amsterdam. The municipality tries to create jobs by devising work-creation schemes. The biggest project is the Bosch Plan: the construction of a nature and recreation terrain south of the city. Between 1934 and 1940, around 20,000 are employed in the creation of Amsterdamse Bos.

Doubled at a Stroke

In 1934, the city launches an ambitious project: a new expansion plan (Algemeen Uitbreidingsplan or AUP). A series of massive extensions to prepare Amsterdam for the year 2000. The black areas on the map are already in place in 1934; the red sections have yet to be built. Urban planning on this scale is still rare. Most of the AUP project is completed after the Second World War.

1938 **First motorway to Amsterdam.**

AUP expansion plan model, c. 1935
Public Works Department

1940–1945

Second World War

On 16 May 1940, German troops enter Amsterdam. In the First World War (1914–1918), the Netherlands remained neutral. This time the country is under occupation for five years. A traumatic period that changes the country, and changes Amsterdam irrevocably.

Racism is a central tenet of the Nazi occupiers. Attacks against Jews escalate in early 1941, culminating in round-ups and deportations: destination unknown. Dutch communists organise a strike in Amsterdam and surrounding towns. The February Strike is the largest public protest against the persecution of Jews in occupied Europe. While the Nazis crush the strike ruthlessly, they adapt their methods and organise the deportation of Jews more efficiently, using Amsterdam's bureaucracy and its records in which all Jews are conveniently registered.

1940 German army invades the Netherlands.

Before the War, **Hollandsche Schouwburg** was a popular theatre in Amsterdam's Plantage district. The Nazis used the building to detain Jews before sending them to Westerbork. Thousands of men, women and children passed through Hollandsche Schouwburg and Westerbork transit camp, to be sent to their death in camps in Eastern Europe. Today, the derelict theatre stands as a monument to the Jews who perished.
→ www.hollandscheschouwburg.nl

Practically the entire Jewish population of Amsterdam is deported to Westerbork, and on to Germany and Poland, there to be killed. Among the victims is Anne Frank. She is 15 when she is sent via Auschwitz to Bergen-Belsen, where she dies in March 1945, shortly before the camp is liberated. Her diary, published later, becomes a powerful indictment against the anti-Semitism of the Nazi period. Sixty thousand Jews from Amsterdam perish: an incredible slaughter and an enormous loss: three-quarters of the Jews of Amsterdam.

On 8 May 1945, Canadian troops enter Amsterdam to liberate the city. The few Jews who return, find their homes stripped bare. The Jewish Quarter, once a symbol of the city's tolerance, is a ghost town.

One Face Representing Millions

Anne Frank and her family are in hiding not far from the museum, at Prinsengracht 263. At the corner, on Westermarkt, is a sculpture of Anne Frank made by Mari Andriessen after the War. The smaller version, the sculptor's working model, is now in Amsterdam Museum.

Anne Frank, 1977
Mari Andriessen (1897–1979)

Tram 8, which runs through the heart of the Jewish part of Amsterdam, is discontinued.

With one exception, to bring Jews to Central Station. And from there to Westerbork. Since the War, no tram 8 has ever appeared on Amsterdam's streets.

LIJN 8 Zuider Amstellaan - Daniël Willinkplein - Van Woustr. - Weesperplein - Weesperstr. - J. D. Meijerplein - Nieuwmarkt - Centr. Station.

Sign for tram 8, c. 1936–'42

1943

On 27 March, a resistance group led by Gerrit van der Veen and Willem Arondeus attack the municipal population registry.

February Strike

Mari Andriessen's *Dock Worker* (the sculptor also made the statue of Anne Frank) commemorates the February Strike of 1941. A burly Haarlem carpenter modelled for the sculptor. He probably also played a part in the resistance. A memorial is held for the strike each year since it was unveiled on Jonas Daniël Meijerplein in 1952.

The Dockworker, 1951
Mari Andriessen
(1897–1979)

Bureaucracy under the Nazis

Following the invasion, the Nazis need information to carry out their plan of annihilation. In May 1941, Amsterdam's civil servants draw up this map for the new regime. Each dot represents ten Jews. It is immediately evident where most Jews live. This map is a vital tool for the Nazis, enabling them to execute their anti-Semitic measures with great precision.

In addition to highlighting resistance to the Nazi regime, the **Resistance Museum** also examines other aspects of the Nazi occupation. A section also looks at the Dutch East Indies. → www.verzetsmuseum.org

VERSPREIDING VAN DE JODEN
OVER DE GEMEENTE (MEI 1941)

CIJFERS IN BLAUW AANTAL JODEN PER BUURT
CIJFERS IN ROOD " NIET-JODEN "
ELKE STIP
10 JODEN

Map showing where Jews live in Amsterdam, 1941

Although the German army agrees to surrender to the Allies on 5 May, some fight on: German snipers fire at a jubilant crowd on Dam Square from the Groote Club on 7 May.

1945

1945–today

1946 Queen Wilhelmina approves an addition to Amsterdam's heraldic emblem: Heroic, Determined, Compassionate.

1951 Work begins on Slotermeer, a new garden suburb.

Capital of Freedom

Few cities can boast as many different nationalities as Amsterdam, around 180 nations are represented. As in previous centuries, migrants arrive from all corners of the world. Many come from neighbouring countries and former colonies: Indonesia, Suriname and the Antilles. Others come as guest workers or as refugees. Everyone has their reason, whether it is love, or work, or the freedom for which Amsterdam is celebrated.

In the 1960s, Amsterdam acquires a reputation as a place where anything and everything goes. A youth group known as Provo challenges the authorities. Not, like in Paris or Berlin, with violence. But with fun and games. In the late 1960s, Amsterdam is a centre of Hippie culture. Drugs are traded openly in the 1970s, and prostitution expands. Women take to the streets to demand their rights, and in 2001, this is the first city to sanction gay and lesbian marriage.

Amsterdam still has a reputation as a free city, though the rules are tighter now. Tolerance and control are delicately balanced. Freedom of religion exists beside freedom of expression. Although the two may conflict fiercely. The murder of publicist Theo van Gogh in 2004 by a religious fanatic puts a major dent in the city's image. Yet Amsterdam is still a place where freedom reigns, at least compared to most other places on the planet. A city's DNA is not that easy to change.

Hippies on Dam Square, at the National Monument, 1970

Make Love, Not War

Hippies from around the world are drawn by Amsterdam's freedom. Dam Square is their favourite place to meet. They play guitar, dance, take drugs and some even camp out around the National Monument. Many older people in Amsterdam view this with disdain. In August 1970, Dutch marines sweep the area clean and the Hippies move to Vondel Park. .

First supermarket opens (Dirk van den Broek). **1953**

1964 First official Turkish guest workers arrive in Amsterdam.

Tolerate or Forbid?

Tolerance is a typically Dutch phenomenon. 'Regulating something that is actually illegal yet which is kind of allowed'. Amsterdam's authorities are adepts of this pragmatic approach. The city has been famous for it since the 1960s. A new phenomenon appears in the 1970s: coffee shops where coffee is hardly drunk at all, but marijuana and hashish are sold and smoked. Soft drugs, prostitution, squatting: all this is allowed in Amsterdam, although within bounds. In this city there is an undefined twilight zone between the permissible and the forbidden.

Tolerance is subject to constantly changing rules. Early in the twenty-first century, tolerance seems to be losing ground. Prostitution may have been legalised in 2000, but in recent years the city has begun to close down brothels in the Wallen neighbourhood. Stricter rules have been imposed on the sale of soft drugs. Squatting, a common phenomenon in the 1980s, is no longer tolerated since 2010. Freedom of thought maybe; freedom of action a little less.

1965 Provo protest movement launched.

Karin Daan's **Homo Monument** on Westermarkt consists of three equilateral triangles of pink granite linked by a line. The monument honours all homosexual men and women who have been or who are persecuted or killed for the nature of their sexuality.
→ www.homomonument.nl

Ajax Players, 1967
Paul Huf (1924–2002)

Wedding of Princess **1966**
Beatrix and Claus
disrupted by smoke
bomb on Raadhuisstraat.

Building begins at **1968**
Bijlmermeer.

Modern Heroes

Four young footballers pose for Paul Huf's camera in
1967. From front to back: Johan Cruijff, Sjaak Swart,
Piet Keizer and Klaas Nuninga. They are the first
eleven's attack formation. Johan Cruijff is acclaimed
Europe's best footballer in 1971, 1973 and 1974. When
this photo is taken, the four are still at the onset of their
amazing career with Ajax.

Riot police blocking the corner of Rokin and Langebrugsteeg,
30 April 1980

1969 Students occupy
Amsterdam University
building (Maagdenhuis).

Squatters Riots

In the 1980s, Amsterdam is the setting for frequent
squatter protests, and the riot squad is often called in
to deal with them. When Beatrix is installed as queen
on 30 April 1980, squatters demonstrate in the streets
chanting 'No house, no crown'. That day the riot squad
has its hands full keeping demonstrators away from
Dam Square, where the royal pageant is played out.

Dapper Market in East Amsterdam has often been acclaimed the country's best
daily market. Not only is the range of produce on sale amazingly diverse, the
people who come there are an astonishing mix as well. Dapper Market attracts
people from around world. www.dappermarkt.nl. → www.dappermarkt.nl

Turkish Schoolgirls, 1987
Marlène Dumas (b. 1953)

A Nice Neat Line

This portrait of a group of Turkish schoolgirls is based on a photo that Marlene Dumas took in Turkey. Amsterdam has many Turkish schoolgirls too: the Turkish community is the largest minority in Amsterdam. For Dumas, the children represent all Turkish school girls, wherever they are in the world. The artist, originally from South Africa, lives and works in Amsterdam.

First coffee shop **1972**
opens: Mellow Yellow.

Demonstrations **1975**
against demolition of
houses in Nieuwmarkt for
the new Metro line.

1980 Riots protesting against coronation ('No house, no crown').

1981 Around 400,000 demonstrators protest against nuclear weapons on Museumplein.

1983 Kerwin Duinmeijer, an Antillean boy aged 15, murdered by a skinhead.

Double Date, Love and Ecstasy, 1996
Micha Klein (b. 1964)

Appearance and Reality

Micha Klein's digital world – colourful, perfect and yet unreal – is full of references to the Flower Power generation of the 1960s and the House scene of the 1990s. Pillman, a happy tablet with arms and legs, symbolises the world of clubs and nightlife in Klein's work.

Amsterdam Civic Guard Portrait, 2001
Henk Schiffmacher (b. 1952) and Aldert Mantje (b. 1954)

Modern Civic Guards

Standing prominently in the centre of this modern civic
guard portrait is the personification of Amsterdam,
with a joint in one hand and Rembrandt's face tattooed
on her breast. She is surrounded by famous Amsterdam
personalities such as Anne Frank, Johan Cruijff and Job
Cohen (mayor of Amsterdam when Theo van Gogh was
killed). Mokum is a popular name for Amsterdam
derived via Yiddish from the Hebrew makom, meaning
'place'.

El Al aircraft crashes in **1992**
Bijlmer on 4 October.

Discover a part of Amsterdam that is changing fast, where
hardly any tourists visit. Catch a ferry from behind
Central Station to North Amsterdam and enjoy a
free ride over the IJ.

2001 In the night of 31 March and 1 April 2001, mayor Job Cohen officiates at the wedding of four gay and lesbian couples at Amsterdam's city hall. Marriage is henceforth open to same-sex couples. These are the first homosexual couples to marry in the world.

Theo van Gogh, 2004
Faith 71 (Donovan Spaanstra, b. 1971)

Frank Wittebrood and Peter Lemke's wedding photo, 1 April 2001. Michael Kooren, Hollandse Hoogte

Frank Wittebrood and Peter Lemke's wedding rings. On loan from Peter Wittebrood-Lemke

Hero or Villain

On 2 November 2004, filmmaker and columnist Theo van Gogh (1957–2004) is murdered on Amsterdam's Linneusstraat. The murderer, religious extremist Mohammed Bouyeri, sees Van Gogh as an enemy of Islam. Others see him as a champion of free speech. That night, the mayor calls for a noise protest on Dam Square. Tens of thousands respond by raising their voices to show their anger.

The Syndics, 2006
Erwin Olaf (b. 1959)

Holland School

Nationale Ballet commissioned photographer Erwin
Olaf to make this group portrait to mark their Holland
School programme. It depicts their six principal
choreographers at that time. Left to right: Hans
van Manen, Ted Brandsen, David Dawson, Toer van
Schayk, Krzysztof Pastor and Rudi van Dantzig.
The composition is inspired by Dutch group portraits
of the seventeenth century.

Work on North/ **2003**
South Line begins.

2008 Amsterdam Internet Exchange is world's largest Internet exchange point.

Tradition and Renewal

Kickboxers from a sport school in Amsterdam's Old West neighbourhood pose either side of William of Orange, father of the nation. By mixing symbols, texts and ornament from different cultures, Arno Coenen references changes in Dutch society. The

Old West, Home's Best, 2007
Arno Coenen (b. 1972)

phrase Determined, Heroic, Compassionate, is from
Amsterdam's heraldic emblem. Moroccan stars
have also been added to the city's flag. Originally,
this tile panel was displayed on an outside wall in
Old West.

Amsterdam's ring
of canals becomes
a Unesco World
Heritage Site.

2010

2012 Amsterdam's 800,000th resident is born.

Amsterdam's Museum Piece

Drugs have been in ample supply in Amsterdam since the 1960s. In the 1970s, the authorities begin turning a blind eye to soft drugs; hard drugs remain illegal. Heroin addicts become a major problem in the 1980s. In recent decades, an enlightened policy of treatment with methadon has significantly reduced the number of addicts. Cannabis (hashish and marijuana) is still widely consumed – in coffee shops and elsewhere.

Joint, 2011

One of the first coffee shops was **Bulldog** (1975) in the Wallen neighbourhood. It soon expanded to form a chain of shops, with one even opening in a former police station on Leidseplein in 1985. That Bulldog had to close in 2013, when new regulations were introduced preventing coffee shops operating too close to schools, in this case Barlaeus Gymnasium.
→ www.thebulldog.com

2013 Willem-Alexander takes the throne.

Illustrations

Photographs from Amsterdam Museum: Monique Vermeulen, unless stated otherwise.

BMA archaeological finds from the Bureau of Monuments and Archaeology. Photos by Jerzy Gawronski.

P. 6 Governesses of the Civic Orphanage, 1683, Adriaen Backer (1635/36–1684), SB 4844, on loan from Spirit Foundation. Photo by René Gerritsen, Amsterdam Museum.
P. 9 Shoe, BMA, DA-35.
P. 10 Pilgrim badge, BMA, ROK1-423. • Plaque showing the arms of Amsterdam at Amsterdam Museum, 1681. Bartholomeus Eggers (1627–1692) (sculptor) BA 767.
P. 11 Foundation pile, 681.
P. 12 A Squad of Harquebusiers with two Civic Guard Kings, 1534, unknown artist, SA 7300.
P. 14–15 Skate, BMA, NDK-2895-1; Bone carder, BMA DIEM-310-4; Boat hook, BMA, NES-20; Leather sheath, BMA, NES5-4;
P. 15 Cooking pot, BMA, ARM-124-3; Wooden spoon BMA, ARM-125-1; Pincers, BMA, ROK1-371; Crucifix, BMA, NES-65; Jacks knucklebone, BMA, NDK-2508-3.
P. 18-19 Bird's-Eye View of Amsterdam, c. 1652-1655, Jan Micker (1598–1664), SA 1531.
P. 20 Bird's-Eye View of Amsterdam, 1538, Cornelis Anthonisz (c. 1505–1553), SA 3009.
P. 21 Pieta, c. 1450, unknown artist, BA 3968. • Adoration of the Shepherds, c. 1559, Pieter Aertsen (1507-1575), SA 7255.
P. 22 William of Orange, c. 1582, Naar Adriaen Thomasz Key, SA 24242. • Fernando Alvarez de Toledo, Duke of Alva, second half 16th century, unknown artist, SA 24436. Photo by René Gerritsen, Amsterdam Museum.
P. 23 Thomas Gerritsz Doesburch, Claesje Hendricksdr Roeclaes and their two Daughters, 1559, attributed to Jacob

War II (d. 1568), 401, on loan from Royal Museum of Fine Arts, Antwerp. Photo by Hugo Maertens, KMSK © Lukas-Art in Flanders. • Relief on Civic Orphanage gate on Kalverstraat, 1581. Joost Jansz. Bilhamer (1521–1590) (sculptor). BA 763
P. 24 Interior of the Oude Kerk, 1661, Emanuel de Witte (c. 1617–1692), SB 4929, on loan from Cultural Heritage Agency, Rijswijk, Amersfoort.
P. 25 Jan Pietersz Sweelinck, 1606, Gerrit Pietersz Sweelinck (1566–after 1612), SB 6391, on loan from Gemeentemuseum, The Hague. • Allegory of Amsterdam as the Centre of World Trade, 1606, Pieter Isaacsz (1569–1625), 486, on loan from Rijksmuseum Amsterdam. Photo by René Gerritsen, Amsterdam Museum.
P. 26–27 Civic Guardsmen from the Company of Captain Jacob Gerritsz Hoing, 1596, Pieter Isaacsz (1569–1625), SA 7338.
P. 28 VOC plate, c. 1650-1674, KA 16219.
P. 29 Terrestrial globe, c. 1645, Firm of Joan Willemsz Blaeu (1596–1673), KA 14781, acquired with support from Rembrandt Association and Prince Bernhard Fund.
P. 30 René Descartes, 17th or 18th century, Copy after Frans Hals, SA 22659. Photo by René Gerritsen, Amsterdam Museum.
P. 31 Joan Huydecoper van Maarsseveen, 1654, Artus Quellinus (1609–1668), BB 208, on loan from Huydecoper Stichting, Maarssen.
P. 32 Jan Cornelisz Geelvinck, 1646, Cornelis Jonson van Ceulen (1593–1661), SA 7347. • Pieter Pietersz Hasselaer and Aeghje Cornelisdr Hooft, 1611, Cornelis van der Voort

(1576–1624), SB 6432-33, on loan from private collection. • Jacob Jacobsz Bicker and Alida Bicker, 1639-41, Joachim von Sandrart (1606–1688), SA 2078-77. Photos by René Gerritsen, Amsterdam Museum.
P. 33 Pieter Jansz Reael, 1643, Govert Flinck (1615–1660), SB 6325, on loan from Cultural Heritage Agency, Rijswijk, Amersfoort. • Jan Bicker and Agniet de Graeff, c. 1663–64, Jan Lievens (1607–1674), after Wallerand Vaillant, 1623–1677, SA 7267-68. • Hiob de Wildt, 1640, Dirck van Santvoort (1610–1680), SB 6396, on loan from Cultural Heritage Agency, Rijswijk, Amersfoort.
P. 34 Governesses and Matrons of the Spinhuis, 1638, Dirck van Santvoort (1610–1680), SA 7402..
P. 35 Registration of the Poor and Orphans at the Almshouse, 1626, unknown artist, SA 3021.
P. 36 Allegory of the Care of Lepers and Innocents, c. 1675, Gérard de Lairesse (1641–1711), SA 7360.4. • Model of the new Town Hall on Dam Square, 1648, Jacob van Campen (1595–1657), design, KA 12023.
P. 37 Dam Square, 1675, Abraham Storck (1644–1708), SA 1755. Photo by René Gerritsen, Amsterdam Museum. • Allegory of the Expansion of Amsterdam, c. 1663, Nicolaes Berchem (1620–1683), SA 2079, A. van der Hoop bequest.
P. 38 The Herengracht Bend, 1685, Gerrit Berckheyde (1638–1698), SB 6406, on loan from Rijksmuseum Amsterdam.
P. 39 Daniel Bernard, 1669, Bartholomeus van der Helst (1613–1670), 402, on loan from Museum Boijmans Van Beuningen, Rotterdam.
P. 40–41 The Gouden Leeuw on the IJ, 1686, Willem van de Velde II (1633–1707), SA 7421.
P. 42 Embarkation of Company Troops at Montelbaan Tower, 1682, Abraham Storck (1644–after 1704), SA 21, acquired with support from Rembrandt Association.
P. 43 The Shipyard of the Dutch East India Company (VOC), 1696, Ludolf Bakhuizen (1630–1708), SB 2764, on loan from Cultural Heritage Agency,

Rijswijk, Amersfoort. • The Courtyard of Amsterdam's Stock Exchange, c. 1670–1680, Job Berckheyde (1630–1693), SA 3025. • Peter the Great, 18th century, unknown artist, 394, on loan from Rijksmuseum.

P. 44 Silver spice box, 1618, Willem van Wolfswinkel (fl. 1591–1626), KA 15115 • Delftware tulip vase, c. 1700, unknown maker, KA 13052. Photo by René Gerritsen, Amsterdam Museum • Silver funeral shield of the corn meters' guild, 1633, Johannes Lutma I (1584–1669), KB 1378, on loan from Rijksmuseum Amsterdam • Silver pleated dish, 1662, Mijndert Takel (1638–1707), KA 16013;

P. 45 Silver salt cellar, 1643, Johannes Lutma I (1584–1669), KA 8051 • Silver sconce, c. 1680, unknown maker, KA 14155 • Nautilus cup, 1649, Hendrick Bloem (1619–1659), KA 14200 • Mother-of-pearl shell, second half 17th century, Cornelis Bellekin (1615–1696), KA 20835, acquired with support from Rembrandt Association • Turbo shell, second half 17th century, unknown maker, KA 18812.

P. 46 Coin chest and wagon from Amsterdam's bank of exchange, 17th century, KB 1700 and KB 1706, on loan from the Royal Collection, The Hague. • Antonio Lopes Suasso, c. 1685, attributed to Rombout Verhulst (1674–1698), BA 575, S.A. Lopes Suasso-De Bruijn bequest.

P. 47 The Anatomy Lesson of Dr Jan Deijman, 1656, Rembrandt van Rijn (1606–1669), SA 7394.

P. 49 Dolls' house with silver miniatures, c. 1730–1770, KB 3763.

P. 50 Box with two mother-of-pearl shells, engraving 1650–1700, silver 1741, Cornelis Bellekin (1615–1696) and Louis Métayer (fl. 1730–1774), KA 14668.

P. 51 Covered cup with a view of Amsterdam, second quarter 17th century, unknown maker, KB 847, on loan from Amsterdams Historisch Museum Society. • Cup with the Admiraal de Ruyter, second half 18th century, unknown maker, KA 18859.

P. 52–53 View of Houtmarkt, c. 1760–87, Hendrik Keun (1738–1787), SB 6394, on loan from Rijksmuseum Amsterdam.

Photo by René Gerritsen, Amsterdam Museum.

P. 55 Arrival of Napoleon in Amsterdam, c. 1811–12, Mattheus Ignatius van Bree (1773–1839), SA 2122.

P. 56 Dancing round the Liberty Tree on Dam Square, 19 June 1795, Jonas Zeuner (1727–1814), SA 37152.

P. 57 Bust of Napoleon Bonaparte, c. 1808, Antoine-Denis Chaudet (1763–1810), BB 286, on loan from Rijksmuseum Amsterdam.

P. 58 Portrait of Louis Napoleon Bonaparte, 1808, Charles Howard Hodges (1764–1837), 307, on loan from Frans Halsmuseum, Haarlem. • The Keys of the City of Amsterdam, 1811, Diederik Lodewijk Bennewitz (c. 1763–1826), KA 8488, KA 8489, KA 8493.

P. 59 Eagle, 1811, unknown maker, KA 7088.

P. 60 Model of a guillotine, early 19th century, unknown maker, KA 8595.

P. 61 Liberty, Fraternity, Equality, 1795, D.M. Langeveld (publisher), KA 16669.

P. 63 Procession over Hogesluis to the Palace of Industry, undated, unknown photographer, Municipal Archive, Amsterdam.

P. 64 The Construction of Two Gasholders at Hollandsche Gazfabriek on Weteringschans, 1847, Cornelis Springer (1817–1891), SA 866.

P. 65 Model of Sinck's hoist, c. 1860, KA 7816. • Trowel and trowel box, 1867, K 386, K 387, on loan from Heineken Collection, Amsterdam.

P. 67 Construction Site, c. 1890–1910, George Hendrik Breitner (1857–1923), SB 6368, on loan from Rijksmuseum Amsterdam.

P. 69 Mouth of the North Sea Canal at IJmuiden, 1878, Christiaan Dommershuizen (1842–1928), SA 25258.

P. 70 Carved elephant tusks, 1919, 395 and 396, on loan from Rijksmuseum Amsterdam.

P. 71 Post-Mill in the Schinkel Neighbourhood, c. 1900, Piet Mondrian (1872–1944), 315, on loan from Gemeentemuseum, The Hague © 2013. Mondrian/Holtzman Trust c/o HCR International Washington DC.

P. 72 Floor Wibaut, 1934, Tjipke Visser

(1876–1955), DA 158. De Key building society tile panel, 1918 (?), Plateelbakkerij Delft NV, KB 2581, on loan from Woonstichting de Key, Amsterdam. Photo by René Gerritsen, Amsterdam Museum.

P. 73 Destruction and Construction, 1930, Frits Sieger (1893–1990), BA 4113.

P. 75 General Expansion Plan model, c. 1935, Office of Public Works, KA 18059.

P. 77 Statue of Anne Frank, 1977, Mari Andriessen (1897–1979), 390, on loan from Anne Frank Foundation.

P. 78 The Dockworker, 1951, Mari Andriessen (1897–1979), BA 3268. Tram 8 sign, c. 1936-42, 180.

P. 79 Map of Jewish Population, 1941, Beeldbank WO2-NIOD.

P. 81 Hippies at Dam Square, 1970, Photo by Ger Dijkstra, National Archive, Spaarnestad.

P. 83 Ajax Players, 1967, Paul Huf (1924–2002), MAI, 391 on loan from Bonny Huf.

P. 84 Riot Squad on Rokin, 30 April 1980, Ino Roël, Municipal Archive, Amsterdam.

P. 85 Turkish Schoolgirls, 1987, Marlene Dumas (b. 1953), 399, on loan from Stedelijk Museum Amsterdam.

P. 86 Double Date, Love and Ecstasy, 1996, Micha Klein (b. 1964), A 41379.

P. 87 Amsterdam Civic Guard Portrait, 2001, Henk Schiffmacher (b. 1952) and Aldert Mantje (b. 1954), 389, on loan from Mobile Arts.

P. 88 Wedding of Frank Wittebrood and Peter Lemke, 1 April 2001, Michael Kooren, Hollandse Hoogte. • Frank Wittebrood and Peter Lemke's wedding rings, 309, on loan from Peter Wittebrood-Lemke. • Theo van Gogh, 2004, Faith 71 (Donovan Spaanstra, 1971), SA 56601. Photo by René Gerritsen, Amsterdam Museum.

P. 89 The Syndics, 2006, Erwin Olaf (b. 1959), 400, on loan from Studio Erwin Olaf.

P. 90–91 Old West, Home's Best, 2007, Arno Coenen (b. 1972), 397, on loan from Rijksmuseum Amsterdam, gift of Paradiso Foundation and Art and Public Space Foundation. Photo from Rijksmuseum Amsterdam.

P. 92 Joint, 2011, DNA 05.1.

© 2013 Uitgeverij Bas Lubberhuizen / Amsterdam Museum

Text by Laura van Hasselt, with Norbert Middelkoop,
Bert Vreeken and Anna Koldeweij
Introduction by Paul Spies
Translation by Sam Herman
Editing by Anneke van de Kieft, Marianne Tieleman and
Monique den Ouden
Illustrations edited by Joyce Edwards and Esmée Heil
Book design by Yolanda Huntelaar, Werkplaats Amsterdam
Printing by Drukkerij Mart.Spruijt, Amsterdam

Tour routes by Nikki Pootjes with Anna Foulidis
and Annemarie de Wildt
Infographics by Kossmann.dejong and Werkplaats Amsterdam
Photography by Amsterdam Museum (unless otherwise
indicated in credits)

All illustrated objects are from the Amsterdam Museum
collection, unless stated otherwise.

ISBN 9789059373624
NUR 693

www.lubberhuizen.nl
www.amsterdammuseum.nl